MW01286225

"I only smoke when I drink..."

Easy ways to have hard conversations as a life agent.

By Michael Bonilla, CPCU

Contents

Copyright 2019

About the Author

Believe it or not this section is always the hardest for me to write about. I really don't enjoy talking about myself. I enjoy having people talk about themselves. What do people want to know about an author? Background? Experiences? Belief systems? I enjoy breaking things and putting them back together. What kind of person am I? What kind of person do I want to represent?

Let me tell you a brief story that tells you what kind of person I am. Back in the early 90's I was sketching out my design for a boxcar derby car for boy scouts. This was my first race and I couldn't think of the type of car I wanted to build. To say the least there was zero inspiration. I scribbled out some designs on this piece of paper and eventually after running out of paper went into the den to find more paper. I stopped for a second and glanced over by the window. After staring out of the window for a second (maybe several minutes) I saw my father as he was pulling into the driveway with his 1990 White Dodge diesel, you could hear it for miles.

Then it hit me. What if I used his truck as the design? I re-read the instructions and rules for the derby. The boxcar kit came in a small cardboard box with a block of wood we could use to make our cars. The instructions read as follows:

- Must have 4 wheels
- Must weigh X LBs, no more and no less.
- Must be X inches long by X Inches wide.

So, that being said. Nowhere in the rules/instructions did it specifically say "this boxcar must be a car". So, for the first time in the boxcar derby history. Michael Bonilla entered a truck. To which everyone started laughing. It was a small wooded version of a 1990's Dodge Ram 2500. With a big Pepsi decal on the driver side door. So, we called it the Pepsi truck.

I placed my 'car' on the race line for the first race and hoped for the best. The judges looked at it. It met the weight requirements, the size requirements and had the appropriate amount of wheels. So, we raced and I waited with anticipation for the results. As I was short I couldn't even see the race. All I heard was, "Pepsi truck 1st place." After all 5 races that day I kept hearing those same words over and over again.

After sweeping that year's event. The following year I decided to change it up and make a replica of the Mach 5 Speed Racer Car, in which I came in third place. That next year every 'car' was a truck, besides mine. Don't bend the rules, don't break the rules, test the rules and test the boundaries of the game you are given. Look for loopholes and exploits in the system.

I'm unsure what kind of insight that might have provided. Nevertheless, this book is the longest, most through and probably well thought out I have written to date. I'm an author, a consultant, a former agency owner, an avid golfer, a husband and most importantly someone who enjoys giving back through teaching.

Preface

Thanks for picking up my latest book. Let me ask you, why did you? What prompted you read this book in particular? For me, I read insurance books to learn new strategies, new ways of thinking and sales tips. Selling for me is right up there with breathing, it's essential to life.

The life insurance industry is changing rapidly and disruptive technologies are slowly starting go transform the competitive landscape. Our industry is an enduring sign of the importance of trust during a client's purchase making decision process. As direct writers start to push out the traditional agent model, the trusted advisor will still hold a seat at the table of value.

Ultimately, we can do three things in the face of adversity. We can flee, fight or freeze, commonly known as the flight or fight response. I chose to fight, because selling is one of the only scalable professions that doesn't discriminate. This fact is especially true in the insurance industry. No matter your background, education, upbringing, lifestyle, personality and as long as you can get licensed, you just might be able to make a real difference.

"A man (person) is nothing without his education. Because, education is the one thing no one can ever take away from you." – Michael Fichera

Chapter 1: Introduction

Something startled me about four years ago, it was around the time I was just getting ready to warm up my second cup of coffee. I had just sat down at my conference table to begin hour number four of my work day, it was around 9:00am or so. Suddenly, and quiet loudly, I heard a murmur in one of the other rooms of the office. It was a whisper at first, turns out it was more like the clam before the storm. One of my brokers had started to lash out in confusion. "What the heck happened?!?", he proclaimed. After about five minutes or so I decided to investigate. As I peered my head through the doorway all I could see were his hands behind his head and the broker wrought with confusion. I've always found the best conflict resolution strategies to start by asking open ended questions. How's it going in here? Why the concerned look?

Well Mike, for some reason I the life insurance company raised the premium on this quote of $1000 to $5000 per year! Wow. Oaky... what happened? The prospect told me he didn't smoke and the life company rated him as a smoker. Did he tell you he wasn't a smoker? Yeah! Can you walk me through what you said and how you asked the prospect? Well, I asked him if he smoked. No, I mean ask me like I am the prospect sitting in front of you.

Needless to say the broker had asked him but didn't read between the lines. So, I dropped in on the follow up call to the prospect. In the insurance game life is going to throw you some curve balls, it's like we always say... life happens. The follow up call (offer presentation) went something like this. Hi Bob, great news the life insurance company ended up making you an offer. Bob, I'm curious though. Can you talk to me about how the medical exam went? Bob, you mentioned to me that you weren't a smoker. To which Bob replied, I'm not a smoker. Well, then what happened with the medical exam? The nurse reported you as a smoker to the insurance company and rated you accordingly. Bob replied, "Well, you asked me if I was a smoker on the application and I said no." A smirk came across my face as I looked over at the broker. When the Paramedical examiner arrived she asked me if I ever smoke and I told her only at parties and only when I drink at parties. I'm only a casual smoker and rarely smoke, maybe a few times a month. Ah... of course.

What do you suppose it takes to sell life insurance? In my estimation selling insurance, especially life insurance relies heavily on your ability to hold a conversation. There are many great 'sales strategies' to latch on to, but ultimately how well can you hold a conversation? When selling I always found that I'd rather have a conversation as opposed to giving a formal 'presentation'. Selling is essentially a search for the truth and should be a reciprocal back and forth process. Selling should be a conversation where we ask a lot of powerful questions and exchange ideas.

Purpose Driven Life Sales

There are around 1,000,000 licensed insurance agents in America. What makes you different? Most sales agents are going to shop the market and attempt to save you money. Ultimately, to sell on value our purpose needs to be developing customized plans (solutions) to meet our client's needs/wants. That being said, as you go on to read this book, think a lot about your purpose and your value as an agent. What are we in the business of doing? What did we sign up for? Are we in the business of shopping around for cheap prices or in the business of protecting families and providing peace of mind? Here is a little fill in the blank.

"I'm in the business of _____"

Consultative, Relationship and Transactional Life Sales

There are fundamentally three types of insurance sales people. There are consultative sales approaches, which are based on qualifying and meaningful conversations. There are sales people who lead with relationships, which are based on who you would rather do business with? There are transactional sales approaches, which are a lot like making pasta, throw it at the wall and whatever sticks it sticks. In this book expect us to talk mostly about how to be a consultative sales agent. Or what I means to be a consultative life agent.

Often I like to have Agents describe to me their role or what they do specifically. The answer typically gives away what kind of producer I'm speaking with. It often goes something like this:

Transactional: "I sell insurance."

Consultative: "I protect families by designing customized life insurance solutions…"

Relationship: "I'm there insurance guy or the person they trust with their insurance."

"The competitor to be feared is one who never bothers about you at all, but goes on making his own business better all the time." – Henry Ford

Chapter 2: Life Insurance Sales Process

What is the most common insurance sales process? Pick a big round number and throw a line out for the client. Do you ever wonder why so many policies just have $500,000 or $1,000,000 death benefits? How about what a lot of new agents do? 'Quote, copy and prey.' Great sales processes tend to be the simplest sales processes. In this chapter we are not going into deep water, it's more of an overview.

A Doctor's Sales Process

I've always thought that a doctor has the best sales process in the world. Why? Well, think about it for a second. What happens when you go to the doctor office? You show up and fill out some initial paperwork (Fact Finder). After filling out the fact finder you sit around for a few minutes and then go into a room and wait for the doctor. The doctor comes in all ready knowing why you showed up (from the answers on the forms). I don't know about your doctor, but mine doesn't tend to barge in with a solution in hand before we start to have a conversation. Most of the time the doctor will ask me an open ended question, "What's going on?" Or, "What brings you by today?" Once the client (patient) explains the perceived reason for being there, the doctor asks some follow up questions and probes a bit.

Ideally, the doctor at this point then would talk about the problem and also talk about possible solutions. Well, we can do surgery or Physical therapy or take meds... The doctor can prescribe a generic pill or a brand name pill. Ultimately, the doctor is convincing you what you need to fix your problem. If the doctor did not instill certainty in their recommendation, what happens? You don't take the meds and or you end up getting a second opinion. Sound like a salesman? It sure does to me. Why do people get second opinions? Because, they don't trust their doctor. You are their insurance doctor, act like it.

I've had few doctors immediately try to prescribe a solution before learning what the problem might be, and asking follow up questions. Usually, the new doctors tend to throw pills around like candy and quick solutions. It's not a feeling that exudes confidence.

Sales Process in a nutshell

1. Set the Stage
   a. Expectations for the process
   b. Sell yourself
   c. Sell the Process
   d. Basic Rapport Building
2. Needs Analysis
   a. Do they need guidance on a death benefit?
   b. If yes, explain the process.
   c. If no, skip step 3.
3. Determine a Death Benefit
4. Submit Application
   a. Set up the Para Medical Exam
   b. Contingent Insurance Receipt (Get the check)
5. Wait for Offer
6. Sell the Offer and Deliver Policy

How to calculate a death benefit.

There are two ways to calculate a death benefit

for a client, we can either use a subjective or objective method. In my approximation we should treat every client equally and the best way to do that is by having a replicable system. So, how do we do that? Easy, let's take a look at a few systems.

- **DIMES**
- *LIFE*
- *Human Life Value Approach*

  For the purposed of this book we are going to look at one of the three.

DIMES

The DIMES system has five essential elements for determining a death benefit. It's vitally important to understand that with any system it's a conversation and **not an interview**. There is not perfect order to ask these questions, so don't force the conversation points.

It goes as follows:

- Debt (D)
- Income (I)
- Mortgage (M)
- Education/Emergency (E)
- Savings Fund (S)

Debt

- Our there outstanding debts? Student loans? Credit Cards? (Not a literal question)

Mortgage

- Do you own this home? (Re-phrase not meant to be literal)
- If something were to happen to you how much would it take today to pay off the mortgage?

Education/Emergency

- Do you want your kids to attend Harvard or Yale? Stole this from Shawshank Redemption.
- What do you think it costs to attend college these days? If you were to guess?
    - What about when Billy turns 18 in 2035?

Savings Fund

Recap (Follow up Questions)

- Based on what **YOU TOLD ME** your need is... BLANK. It's important that the insured comes up with the number. It's their number, not my number.

Other Follow Up Questions

- Do you have any insurance at work?
  - i. I know it's cheap but the thing about it is that you don't own it and the company can change the benefit. The company owns the policy. It's kind of like renting versus owning.
- Do you have other assets that you are going to pass along?
- Here our options we can put you in a temp plan 10/20/30. The great thing about temp insurance is that it's inexpensive but its temp.
  - i. This opens up permanent options as well.

QERC Sales System

This is a sales system that I created about 3 years ago or so, while I was watching my favorite movie My Cousin Vinny. It's called the QERC system. It's a rather simple and to the point system to help new agents.

- Question (Open)
- Educate
- Recommend
- Close (with a question)

The first step is to open with a question. The best openings start with an open ended question. Why? Telling is not selling. Once you've gotten the client's attention or curiosity they will follow you down the rabbit hole. This could be one of your transitions or an interesting statistic and or a factoid in the form of a question.

The second step is to use the answer form the prospect and take that an educational opportunity to further the process. Education is the cornerstone of any good sales process. It's the foundation we build our houses on. This part of the process is basically putting the ball on the tee.

The third step of the process is to make our professional recommendation. The three most powerful words for a new agent are, "As your agent..." As your agent I recommending going with X, because of Y and Z.

The last step in the process is simply just to close by asking another question. If you are recommending LTC on a life policy, "Is that something you want coverage/protection for?"

I get a lot of flack about this part of the system

from agents. But Mike, why should you ever ask, just put it on the policy? Because, selling isn't telling. My recommendation means something, but I want the client to think about what I'm recommending and they can now make an informed decision to reduce chargebacks and shopping.

Developing Urgency

Urgency is one of the key principles of selling, one of the pillars of a good sales process. Life insurance isn't something you can just put on hold and wait to get some day. We don't know when our time is up in this world, we have no clue. Heaven forbid you walk out of my office and get hit by a bus, how will your family get by? (Not a literal question, this is the perception I want to suggest during the conversation)

- (Heaven forbid) If something were to happen to you today, walking out of this office. What would it take to pay off the remainder of your mortgage, roughly speaking?

Where in the above statement did we attempt to develop urgency? "If something were to happen to you **today**, walking out of this office." Every statement has a purpose, we have to plant seeds of doubt that highlights the importance of not putting off an important part of your life, protecting your family from financial devastation. The longer you wait the more expensive it becomes. Remember, selling is not telling, use a question to develop urgency.

"Success is walking from failure to failure with no loss of enthusiasm." – Winston Churchill

Chapter 3: Life Statistics

As we discuss life insurance and sales, it is important to have a very good understanding on the following facts and statistics. About 70% of consumers are prompted by agents to pursue some kind of life insurance quote. Why? Because, people often do not want to ponder their own death and need guidance. It's generally not a happy thought.

As part of being an educator we must first become educated. If you are new to the industry and happen to be looking for 'an in' so to speak, you need to learn your stuff. Life insurance factoids can be interesting segways or conversation starters. This is especially true when talking to large groups of people. Let me ask you something, what is the average life need in your state? What is the average life policy face amount? How many people are uninsured or need more insurance?

One of my colleagues sent me this interesting article on WebMD written by Katherine Kam and I wanted to pull this expert, "In a national 2004 study published in Circulation, researchers at the University of California, San Diego, and Tufts

University School of Medicine examined 53 million U.S. death certificates from 1973 to 2001. **They discovered an overall increase of 5% more heart-related deaths during the holiday season.** When researchers looked at individual years, they found varying increases in cardiac deaths for every holiday period they studied, except two."

Life Insurance Statistics

1. Most industry experts recommend a death benefit of 8 to 12 times your annual income.
2. 59% of households have no individual life insurance at all.
3. 44% of households believe they need more life insurance
4. 33% of homes would have trouble paying bills if the primary earner passed away.
5. The average amount of life insurance in America is only $167,000.
6. The average person 40 to 55 has a mortgage debt of $200,000.
7. 1 in 4 people say they need more life insurance.

8. 3 in 10 Americans have no life insurance.

9. 8 in 10 Americans overestimate the cost of life insurance.

California Fact Sheet 2018 pulled from the ACLI

Jobs

- The life insurance industry generates approximately 225,600 jobs in California, including 81,500 direct employees and 144,100 non-insurance jobs.
- 417 life insurers are licensed to do business in California and 11 are domiciled in the state.

Protection

- California residents have $3.7 trillion in total life insurance coverage.
- State residents own 10 million individual life insurance policies, with coverage averaging $244,000 per policyholder.
- Group life insurance coverage amounts to $1.3 trillion.
- Individual life insurance coverage purchased in California in 2016 totaled $222 billion.

- $38 billion was paid to California residents in the form of death benefits, matured endowments, policy dividends, surrender values, and other payments in 2016.
- Annuity benefits paid in the state in 2016 totaled $8 billion.

Investments

- Life insurance companies invest approximately $765 billion in California's economy.
- About $585 billion of this investment is in stocks and bonds that help finance business development, job creation, and services in the state.
- Life insurers provide $96 billion in mortgage loans on farm, residential, and commercial properties, and own $12 billion in real estate in California.

ACLI in California

- 235 ACLI member companies provide financial and retirement security to California families through life insurance, annuities, long-term care and disability income insurance, and retirement plans.

- 95 percent of all life and annuity payments are from ACLI members.
- 90 percent of total life insurance coverage is provided by ACLI members.

Across America
- 90 million American families rely on life insurers' products for financial and retirement security.*
- Life insurers are leading providers of retirement solutions, including 401(k)s, 403(b)s, 457s, IRAs, and annuities, managing 18 percent of all defined contribution plan assets and 14 percent of all IRA assets.
- More than 16 percent of Americans' long-term savings is in permanent life insurance and retirement annuities.
- Life insurers pay out $1.7 billion to families and businesses every day.
- Life insurers invest $6.4 trillion in the U.S. economy—95 percent of the industry's total assets.

- Life insurers are a major source of bond financing for American businesses, holding almost 22 percent of all U.S. corporate bond.

*75 million households rely on life insurance and/or non-qualified annuities; an additional 15 million households who don't own life insurance or non-qualified annuities rely on qualified annuities, disability income insurance, long-term care insurance, supplemental insurance, or a combination of these products.

Sources: ACLI calculations based on National Association of Insurance Commissioners (NAIC) 2016 annual statement data; U.S. Bureau of Economic Analysis, 2016 data; U.S. Census Bureau, 2016 data; U.S. Bureau of Labor Statistics, 2016 data; U.S. Treasury Department, 2016 data; and 2016-2017 MacroMonitor Survey data.

"How often have I said to you that when you have eliminated the impossible, whatever remains, however improbable, must be the truth? – Sherlock Holmes

Chapter 4: Root Cause Problem Solving and Life Sales

What is root cause problem solving? Otherwise known as RCA or Root Cause Analysis is the method of determining an underlying problem. For instance, picture if you would a house. Now picture rain clouds above the house. Now picture a house in the rain. But, for some reason there is a hole in the siding of the house, from general damage. From that hole in the house, water begins to flow out of the house. What is the problem? It's obvious that there is a hole that needs to be plugged in the wood siding, right? Well, what happens when the hole is plugged? The waters stops flowing out of the hole. It also starts to fill the house up with water. The underlying problem or root cause would be that there is a hole in the roof or chimney.

My Clients Keep Cancelling On Me... HELP!

What is the problem? The problem is that my clients are cancelling on me, right? No, wrong. That is the symptom of the problem. Life insurance involves a lot of 'framing' or pre-framing, if you will. What I mean is that as the agent it is our job to do two things. Plant seeds in the clients head and qualify. What do I mean by that? Well, our job is to make sure the client understands in the beginning (of the process) that this life policy that they are buying is meant to be kept a long time. Make sure they can afford it even if times get tough. If not, lower the premium to something they feel they are comfortable with. So, what is the root cause problem? The problem is that as an agent you are either not qualifying enough or not setting up expectations. If you ever think about cancelling this policy, give me a call.

I'm running into a lot of objections... HELP ME!

We'll touch specifically on objections later on in this book. Ultimately, what I want you to think about is this simple question, "Who would you rather do business with?" Every encounter you have with a prospect you want them to think about and provide an answer to this question. Remember Bob Burg said it best, 'All things being equal people tend to do business with those they know, like and trust.'

I'm not getting enough referrals... What's going on??!?!?

How are you asking? What's your system? Do you ask? Do you ask often? How many times do you ask? What's your script look like? Do you feel uncomfortable asking for a referral? If so, why? Theoretically, every person you talk to is a person you can most likely genuinely help. Old school referral systems tend to be hit or miss, try aggressively developing your clients instead. Follow up with clients with text messaging campaigns to check in on important dates.

I can't seem to get referral partners to reciprocate... why?!?!

What's your system? Do you offer incentives for referrals? Do you show up? Do you put in the work? Are you stopping by and dropping off gifts? Our firm went to the extent of delivering floral arrangements with a customized logo on the vase for key referral partners. Do you reciprocate referrals back to the referral partner? Often these arrangements tend to become somewhat lopsided relationships, why? I think the reason why that happens is the fact we don't set proper expectations and truly take the time to understand what the other person is looking for in the relationship.

When do I know a client is a term or perm client?

This is actually one of the most common questions new agents have. When do I know a client is a term or perm client? How do we know when to pitch a far more expensive permanent solution over term insurance? It's a great question. The answer depends on the situation. In some situations, such as estate planning, term insurance is simply not an option. The easiest way is to ask the client how long they want coverage for, and then throw a line out for permanent.

If you are representing a single company and looking at a replacement policy, why not just pitch the permanent option? Let's say a client comes in with a $500,000 dirt cheap 10 year term policy, knowing that you are going to lose on price by a mile, why not present an alternative solution? I didn't often compete on price, normally I assumed most clients would end up paying more (mostly due to the increased coverage amounts) about 90% of the time. If you do compete on price, think of it like Monopoly, 'Don't collect $200 and go straight to Permanent Insurance.'

My rates are not competitive so customers pre-shop me!

What is the problem? You are getting shopped? No, that's too easy. The symptom is shopping, because you didn't close the para medical exam. How did you establish yourself as an expert? How did you instill certainty in the client? Why do people get second opinions for everything? Trust was not established. How did you convince the insured that **NOW** was the time to buy? Did you possibly provide too many options in your recommendation?

Prospects keep telling me that, 'they want to think about it.'

This is actually one of the most common objections. Why? Because, it's ambiguous. What do most people instinctively use as a rebuttal... "Well Prospect, what do you have to think about?" This is actually a decent question, but it's not that effective asa rebuttal. Why do people give this objection? It's rather simple, because you didn't instill a sense of urgency in the prospect to sign up now. What you're probably not doing is asking this question, "Have you shopped for insurance in the past?" and "If so, why didn't you sign up at that time?" and or "What would your key considerations to think about when making a purchase as important as life insurance?" Find ways to repackage objections into qualifying questions and magically you'll find most objections get prevented. Who would've thought?

I can't beat cheap policies... what do I do?

Why can't you beat cheap policies? The problem is that you think you have to compete on price, because life insurance is a commodity, right? The problem is your process. The problem is that somewhere in your process the client is not certain and a process that lacks certainty leads to objections. Somewhere in your process you did not shift the focus from price to value. Well, how do we do that? Simple, buy my next book. Just kidding. Who controls the conversation? Who is the expert? Who makes the recommendation? Does the client make the professional recommendation?

Check the box

The following topics need to be boxes checked throughout your sales process.

- Sell Yourself
    - Why should someone buy from you and not a computer?
- Sell your Company
    - Why should someone trust your company with protecting their family?
- Sell the Product
    - Why this product? Why does this product fit my needs?
- Sell the Process
    - Why should I wait and not get a non-medical policy?
- Sell the Concept
    - Why should I purchase mortgage protection? Etc.

Why? Because, people need to be certain of the person they choose to do business with. Well Mike, what about… Would you buy insurance from a person who recently committed a felony? Exactly. Some life agents like to think that for some reason we are not sales people, unless you get paid just to educate prospects you are a salesperson. You can make your title sound as fancy as you'd like, if you get paid on commissions you are a sales agent.

"Prospecting – find the man with the problem." –
Ben Friedman

Chapter 5: Prospecting Ideas

Let me ask you something. Let's suppose this year you've written about 100 life contracts, how many clients do you have? For every client you acquire you should attempt to get three referrals. Who is a possible life insurance client? Anyone from the time they are born up until the die they die, more or less. If there is a willing prospect there might be a market for them. When prospecting make sure to prospect within your wheel house.

Prospecting Ideas

Sandwiched Families

What is a sandwiched family? A sandwiched family is a middle generation household simultaneously responsible for taking financial care for both a younger and older generation. Almost 50% of Americans aged 40 to 59 fall into a sandwiched category.

Conversion Opportunities

Theoretically, all life insurance contracts are convertible. The easiest target are expiring term insurance policies and attempting to convert into permanent insurance. If you are an existing agent this is the lowest hanging fruit for your book of business.

Divorce Lawyers and Estate Planners

Want an easy way to serve and underserved community of people? Focus on networking with divorce attorneys. Why? Because, when a couple gets divorced in some states the court will require and impose life insurance on the breadwinner. One of my best referral partners was a successful Los Angeles Family Law Attorney. Clients who hire an attorney have disposable income, for the most part. Why? Because, lawyers are expensive and that means they have assets worth fighting over. As a life agent you can bridge the divide and protect those assets. Needless to say when a couple gets divorced one of the two people was probably exclusively responsible for handling the insurance for the entire household. That means, the person man/woman who was not handling the insurance gets an education really quick about what they do not know about insurance.

Board of Directors

Most people overlook the power of board seats and the good will it buys you as a sales professional. Now, there are legal liabilities to consider when joining a board of directors position and it requires a lot of volunteer hours. Don't join a board just to join a board or with gaining new business as the sole purpose.

Your Own Book of Business

Don't overlook your own book of business. My in-laws often complain about how their State Farm agent only calls to try and sell them life insurance. A broken clock is right twice a day, one day might just be the right day for them to buy life insurance from him. There is a reason why State Farm sells the most life insurance, they tend to ask a lot. Run lists of auto/no life or home/no life. Or run lists of expiring term policies and or aging clients.

Funeral/Wedding List

A funeral/wedding list is a list of people that you would like to attend either event. For me, being recently married this was an easy one to accomplish. Ideally, starting in the industry from scratch, it helps to have a list of at least 200 prospects to reach out to in your 'warm' market.

Warm Market

Do your friends, family and neighbors know that you are in the insurance industry? A warm market is like a gold mine for insurance agent. Why? Because, this is all low hanging fruit for you. Try this wild strategy it's called, 'Go outside and talk with your neighbors'.

Single people

Don't ignore or assume someone doesn't need/want life insurance until you have actually confirmed that. Why would a single person need life insurance? Because, they are thinking about their future? Because, they have debt? Because, they have a favorite charity. Not all single people are going to be wanting to buy life insurance, in fact most will probably not be interested.

- If something were to happen to you who would pay off your student loans?
    - o Single parents or moms will be serious life insurance company, because they care.

"Make a customer, not a sale." – Katherine Barchetti

Chapter 6: Life Transition Statements

What is a transition? A transition is merely the statement or question we use to move from one product or topic to the next. These transitions will vary from life-only to multi-line agents, use what works and discard the rest.

Types of Transitions

General

- By the way who is your life insurance currently with?
- Who's your life insurance with? (Is that important to you?)
- How much life insurance coverage do you have to protect your family? Would it surprise you to know that about 50% of my clients end up paying nothing out of pocket for their long term care insurance?
  - o Using a simple strategy.
- Heaven forbid if something were to happen to you how much would your family need each year to maintain the same standard of living

and how much would you need to give them a higher standard of living. How olds your youngest and set up your income replacement for 20 years.

- Now that we have insured your assets, let's talk about what is truly important, what's protecting your loved ones from financial ruin? Have you ever thought about mortgage protection insurance? (Cheesy old school transition)
- Have you ever thought about life insurance?
- If I could better protect your family would you consider buying better life insurance?
- How much life insurance coverage do you have to protect your family?

Homeowners

- Can your spouse pay off the house if you pass away? (That way you don't have to give the house back to the bank or move.)
- If something would happen to you would you like your family to pay off the house?
- Have you ever thought about mortgage protection insurance?

Business Owners

- What type of succession plan do you have in place?
  - o What can you tell me about it?
- Who are your key employees? The kind that are irreplaceable?
  - o What kind of plan do you have in place to protect your business in case something should happen to them?

Multi-line Agent

- I noticed you don't have life insurance with us who's it with?
- Have you met with our agency's life insurance specialist?
- Have you taken advantage of you free life insurance reviews?
- Did you know our company offers an auto discount if you also have life insurance? (With the company)
- Prospect, when was the last time you got your blood tested or had a check-up? (Never used myself but heard it works from a successful broker, target is 50 YO men)

"The harder the conflict, the more glorious the triumph." – Thomas Paine

Chapter 7: Life General Sales Tips

Selling life insurance is all about developing an activity driven life process and providing a consultative touch. The more active you can be the more people you will talk to and statistically speaking about 70% of consumers who purchase life insurance are prompted to do so by insurance agents. In this part of the book we are going to discuss some general tips and tricks.

General Sales Tips

Learn to ask Open Ended Questions

My great grandfather was the salesman of all salesman, this guy could sell. He mastered the opened ended question and distilled it down to a simple opener. Every time he would see you it was a simple window into his charm, "How's life?" As you sell learn to master open ended questions.

Have a list. Always have a list that you work.

Every great salesperson needs to have a list to work. Every day. As an agent I made it a point to call around 50 to 200 people per day. If you find yourself underperforming, pick up the phone and start dialing. Smile and dial.

Learn to be interesting

What's the biggest challenge you have when meeting people in networking situations? Well Mike, I'm afraid of being that guy in the corner not talking to anyone. It's a rather easy problem to solve, just be interesting. Well, how do I do that? Great question! It's simple. If you want to be interesting learn to become interested in people. How do we do that? Just start by asking questions about the person. Most people have the same favorite subject matter, themselves. People tend to talk about 4 subjects in life, and only 4 subjects in life. People talk about people, things, ideas and events. Start there.

Learn to Care, but not too much.

Caring is kind of like a drug, in that it's very infectious. People love to be around people who care about them. When people care too much sometimes we can invade boundaries and have the opposite desired effect. He who cares least wins? Wrong, he who is over eager loses.

Learn to time block.

Learn to time block. Why? Because, flying by the seat of your pants only gets you so far as an agent. Stick to a schedule and write it down at the beginning of everyday. Often, we start with good intentions, but someone calls in and something has to get down yesterday and we're off to the races.

Learn to tell stories

When I was growing up I always noticed how my friends who seemed to be the best story tellers seemed to have this magnetism at parties. Ever notice that? Who's the center of attention? Short term, maybe it's the loudest people in the room, but long term it's the people who can tell really good stories.

Learn to pause

I changed this chapter title from 'learn when to shut up' as I felt that was a little too harsh. Ever listen to someone rant on for 5 minutes straight to the point at which they get red in the face from not taking time to breath? It's not a flattering quality for a salesperson and doesn't instill a lot of confidence in the client. If I talked at the same pace I typed I don't think people would give me the time of day. Pausing is a lost art form and has been almost eviscerated from our industry. Pausing is powerful, because it builds tension and is a great way to get the client to act or fill in the gaps. At the very least you can tell if the client is listening and paying attention to your presentation. This begets the old saying, "He who speaks first loses." Along with learning to pause speaking in soft tones at the right moment can be a huge difference maker. Pausing at the very least demonstrated your ability to be perceived as a listener.

Have a consistent script

I'm a movie buff, always have been. When I run sales training events and other learning expos, I often like to start by having the attendees ask each other, "What's your favorite movie?" Why? If we want to be interesting we first must learn to become interested in other people. Another reason I like to start this way is the fact that it lets me easily transition to script building. My favorite movie is either Maltese Falcon, Tremors and or My Cousin Vinny, depends on my mood.

Think of your favorite actor for a second. How many great actors do you think improv lines consistently? Every great actor follows a script and minor lines are sometimes improv. Every great salesperson has and uses a consistent script. Why? Because, consistency produces reliable data and from reliable data we can determine the level of effectiveness of are one liners, questions and closes. If you wing it each time your process is hard to track from a results standpoint. If you wing it, how do you know what specifically worked and what didn't?

Understand your audience

I often break insurance customers down into two broad categories. There are think people and there are feel people. Some people are analytical and some people are emotional based thinkers. This is abundantly clear on news stations where people are 'debating' and one person is using facts and the other emotions. Yet, both people are baffled by the others argument and cannot seem to comprehend a word the other person is saying.

- *Think people tend to gravitate towards numbers, factoids, figures, statistics and interesting math concepts.*
- *Feel people tend to enjoy stories, analogies, anecdotes and parables.*

Why is this important? Well, how you relay information to one of these people might make or break a sale. Have you ever given a dynamite presentation and the prospect says, "I'll think about it." I mean a presentation in which you think you crushed it for an easy layup and shocking the person says no. It happens. Happened to me before I had this new way of looking at customers and then customizing my talk paths accordingly.

Think people will often say, "Let me think about it. Or I think I'm good. Or I think I have enough insurance."

Feel people will do the opposite and say, "I feel..."

"Every sale has five obstacles: no need, no money, no hurry, no desire, no trust." – Zig Ziglar

Chapter 8: Life Objections

Objections are a natural part of doing business. Why? Because, on a daily basis we are bombarded with hundreds if not thousands of advertisements. In this chapter we are going to dig into common objections and strategies to handle those objections. An average client has maybe one or two serious objections and sometimes those objections are just complaints. By in large most objections are similar to buying life insurance.

What causes a client to object?

Objections are mostly caused because we as salespeople did something to cause them. Either one or all of these four things happened during your presentation;

1. We confused the client
2. We didn't explain something well enough
3. We didn't flush out questions and concerns and address them

4. Prospect is not qualified

We (salespeople) either confuse the prospect, don't answer a question and or do not address a concern. Or the prospect is not qualified to buy the product you are trying to sell them.

Typical Objections

Why should I buy life insurance? So, my wife can run off with my best friend and be rich?

Have you ever come across this gem before? Typically, this is an objection that comes from men and is given during the prospecting phase. There isn't much you can do here. What I tend to do is focus on the kids, if there are kids in the home. Try to focus the conversation on what's important to the prospect.

Your Price is too high!

In the absence of value price is primary factor. I'd be lying if I tried to peddle the typical consultant line of price isn't a factor, because it is a big factor in our purchasing decision making. Price doesn't have to be the only factor. Let me ask you a process question. If you are selling temporary insurance, why would you ever present a price before medical underwriting? The price is completely variable and dependent on the blood work and medical history Well Mike, you are so big on conditional receipt of insurance, won't I have to explain the 'down payment' amount for the initial check? All the insurance company is looking for is 10% of the projected premium or a single month of estimated premium, roughly. (Read between the lines)

Remember, price objections often just spring from lack of qualification or lack of demonstrated value.

I need to talk to my wife or husband or partner.

Again, this an objection that was solely because we did not take the time to ask a question during our process. Most new agents make the mistake of asking, "why?" Don't do that, instead repackage the objection as a question for your process. Example: John, do you normally make these decisions alone or do you consult with someone?

I need to talk to my lawyer.

This objection is the same as the one above. Normally, higher profile people have attorneys looking over contracts. It happens.

I have it through work.

What's your natural inclination when a prospect states, "I have it through work? There are two ways to rebut this, either we can take a direct approach or an indirect approach. We can ask a couple of questions.

- "That's great! Why don't we set some time aside this week to review it?" (Sometimes just asking is the best way to go)
- "That's great! When did you get that policy?" (Work policies typically cover a single year's salary)
  - o Do you think/feel that is enough coverage?
- "That's great! Do you know how much coverage is on that policy?" (Most people do not)
  - o Well, why do we sit down to review it?

I don't feel that I need life insurance.

Ever get this beauty? Why do you think this happens? It's simple, a foundation built on sifting soil cannot stand the test of time. This is simply an effect of not inserting meaning into the conversation and or the person doesn't need life insurance. Not every person needs life insurance, believe it or not. Don't fall for the trap of asking, why? Why? Because, then it becomes combative and you are questioning the persons motives. You're just going to put the person on the defense and have them try to justify their reasoning. Uncover reasons to make them care about buying insurance.

I need to talk to my accountant.

Accountants can be your biggest enemy or biggest protractor. Don't try to rebut this, learn to ask the question. Learn to team up with accountants and get them involved in the process.

Don't justify a client's objection

After having a robust back and forth with a life broker, we arrived at somewhat of an impasse. We were talking about the affluent market space and the life broker held this ludacris position that, 'all wealthy people are frugal, because that's often how they became wealthy in the first place.' Insurance agents are great at justifying things. Sometimes we justify our own misconceptions. Our job is to present value and justify the price. Don't categorize all people into the same bucket for purposes to justifying your own lost sales. People are different and will often spend money above their budget if they see the value of doing do.

Rebuttals

When handling objections it's vitally important to not to be combative. Start by just affirming what the prospect is saying and use a simple strategy called '**if we could, would you?'** Example: *John, if we could put together a great policy/package to protect your family, would you give us 15-20 minutes?* Rebuttals don't have to be fancy, sometimes the simpler the better. I know a lot of this may seem a bit cheesy or theoretical, but it works. Have your rebuttals ready, and practice them.

Pre-framing to pre-handle objections

Life insurance isn't something you buy it's something you apply for so the first thing we have to do is apply. I can give you a range of prices but we don't know what the rate will be until you go through underwriting. The next step will be to get you through underwriting and then we can talk about prices available. When people go through the underwriting process there is a good chance they will buy a policy.

"Get busy living or get busy dying." –Steven King

Chapter 9: Life Qualifying Questions

What is qualifying? Qualifying is all about putting yourself in the best possible position to win. Let me ask you something, would you apply for a job that you are not qualified for? Why not? Because, the odds of getting the job are almost nil. Firstly, we want to make sure that before you invest the time to go thru the buying process, that the client is actually qualified and has the intention to purchase the policy. There are two types of qualifying questions. The first are specific close ended questions and the second are open ended value questions.

Close Ended

- Have you previously applied for life insurance?
- Are you familiar with the process?
- Height?
- Weight?
- Do you have any serious medical history in your family?
- Were you looking to purchase today?

Types of qualifying questions

Probing Death Benefit

- Did you know how much insurance you needed? Or were you looking for some guidance?
- Did you have an idea of how much insurance you wanted? Or would you like some guidance?

Current Life Policy Underinsured

- How did you come up with that amount of insurance? (Re-phrase)
- How did you come up with this plan? (Poke a hole in the plan, attack the plan not the price to compete against the current agent, credibility beats price)

Business Owner

- What type of succession plan do you have in place?
  - What can you tell me about it?
- Who are your key employees? The kind that are irreplaceable?

- What kind of plan do you have in place to protect your business in case something should happen to them?

General Asset Annuity Opportunity Probing

- Do you have any other assets that act as life insurance?
- Do you have any assets that you would want to pass along?
- What do you have that acts like life insurance? What I mean is, what do you currently have that if god forbid you were to pass away, would pass on to your loved ones?

Wants Assessment – Price Sensitivity

- Ideally, what would you like your plan to look like?
- Have you ever thought about paying in full for your insurance?

Urgency Seed Planting Question

- If something were to happen to you today, walking out of this office. What would it take to pay off the remainder of your mortgage, roughly speaking?

Death Benefit currently Too low

- How did you come up with that amount of insurance?
- How did you come up with this plan? (Poke a hole in the plan, attack the plan not the price to compete against the current agent, credibility beats price)

Value Question

- How often do you meet with your current agent/broker to make sure your protection meets your current needs? (Use this to dilute their current agents value and assess needs or wants)
- What do you think it costs to attend college these days? If you were to guess?

o What about when Billy turns 18 in 2035?

- Do you have other assets that you are going to pass along?

Other Insurance Questions

- Do you have any insurance at work?
- How long have you had it for?
- What can you tell me about it?

Group Life / Company Policy Rebuttal Questions

- That's great! When did you get that policy? (Work policy)
- That's great! When did you get that policy?"
- "That's great! Why don't we set some time aside this week to review it?"

No time Rebuttal Question

- *John, if we could put together a great policy/package to protect your family, would you give us 15-20 minutes?*

Needs Assessment Probing

- Did you know how much insurance you needed? Or were you looking for some guidance?
- Did you have an idea of how much insurance you wanted? Or would you like some guidance?
- Do you have any other assets that act like life insurance? (That pass along to loved ones)
- Have you ever considered paying for your insurance in full?
- Would you consider paying in full if you could get a significant discount?

"The perennial student is the richest person on earth." – Michael Bonilla

Chapter 10: Life Closes

The best closes from my experience are the simplest closes. Don't overthink your close. Remember, selling is about asking questions so close with a question, not a statement. Closing is not a one and done process. You have to be closing throughout the entire sale. When you open your mouth for the first time people will immediately make a judgement about you and whether or not they want to do business with you. During your process expect to get 'mini' closes that will confirm a commitment along the way.

Ask for permission to ask for the sale. Growing up I was always taught that you never open up another man's refrigerator without asking for permission first. When selling I adopt a similar philosophical approach. How would you like it if someone sat down with you over a cup of coffee and immediately started to sell you something? For me, I would feel a bit taken back. Don't rush the close or the process. When you cook a turkey, do you just stick the turkey in the oven and throw on the heat? No! You have to pre-heat the oven, you have to thaw the turkey and you have to prep the turkey.

Soft Closes or Hard Closes?

Once I had an agent try to hard close me on a life policy for about 20 minutes and let me tell you, from one salesperson to another I'm an easy close, except when it's a hard close. Well Mike, why should you try to go for one of the soft closes like, "Let's just get the application going and see if you qualify for the policy?" Closing should be the easiest part of the process. Closing much like rapport building is a not a one and done processes. You have to close every prospect on; why to buy now, what to buy, the amount of insurance to buy, how to pay and buying from you!

When do you know when to close?

Well the answer is obvious, when I end my presentation, right? How do you know a client is ready to be closed? When they start asking buying questions that is how you know. A close doesn't always have to wait for your presentation to conclude, sometimes people just want a price and want to buy something.

What are buying questions?

A buying question is simply a soft tell that the client wants to buy your product without directly asking to buy. For instance, "How much does something like this cost?" Or for example, "Can I pay every month or all at once?" A prospect asking about payment plans is ready to go, generally.

Design your close

What's the most important part of a trial? The opening statement and the second most important part for an attorney is the closing statement. How do you close? What do you say? This is my favorite role playing conversation to have with salespeople. Close me on X. Pitch me X. My close is probably the simplest and most assumptive, "How would you like to pay?" Some agents do a Ben Franklin close, or a three option close or a 'good, better and best' close. Whatever is congruent with your style of selling, design a close and stick to it. Remember, there is no such thing as a good deal for the wrong insurance policy.

"The art of being wise is the art of knowing what to overlook."- William James

Chapter 11: Life Sales Mistakes

If a consumer says that they cannot buy the product because of X, then have your rebuttals ready. Don't let objections get in the way of your flow and presentations. Objections are part of the process don't be afraid to handle them. Embrace objections and chalk them up to moments of learning. Objections are great ways to learn about your own process. People really enjoy buying stuff, surprisingly what they do not enjoy is being sold.

At some point it's paramount you establish a budget and a desire to allocate some of that budget to protection something.

- Don't get in your own way.
- Too many choices and offers.
- Set yourself up for success, not failure.
- Don't shy away from tough conversations.
- Don't let your gut be your only guide, stick to a process.
  Don't give up on someone.

- Don't be afraid to say that you do not know the answer, be the person who is known to be unrelenting and resolute to finding the answer.
- Not investing in internet leads.
  - o I've worked internet leads just like everyone else. I fully understand the marketplace of internet lead companies, but some are good leads.

Presenting too quickly

Don't present too soon. One of my life altering pieces of pop-culture, life defining even, when Paul Walker races Vin Diesel in Fast and the Furious. That first quarter mile race, what happened? Paul Walker came in a close second, but he hit the Nitrous Oxide too soon. What was the lift lessoned learn? Three unforgettable words as Paul Walker starts to pass Vin Diesel at the end of the race, "Too soon junior!" Don't rush into your own presentation, take your time.

Being a road warrior I live out of Starbucks and Panera Breads. On one Tuesday morning while mulling over a spreadsheet and enjoying a wet cappuccino, I witnessed one of these, 'Too Soon Junior" type of moments. A well-dressed life agent from a large firm, a multi-level type of firm, ambushed a completely unexpected prospect. Here is basically what happened. The broker showed up a couple minutes a head of the client, I tend to notice other insurance people. The broker takes a seat at a table, right across from mine. The prospect walks into the meeting dressed quite casually and does the awkward look-around and waive. The broker and client engaged in the typical small talk for a couple of minutes and out of nowhere this broker launches into his shtick. For about 15 or 20 minutes the broker didn't skip a beat, nor did he bother to ask any real questions. Asking, "Does that make sense?" does not qualify as a substantive question in my book. Questions should not be superficial book ends for your sales process. Questions should be questions, in that the question is used to gather information to make adjustments to your process. The prospect looking clearly lost in the broker's presentation, began to show physical signs of distress. To which, the broker did not adjust or take the time to check rapport.

Why do you think that was? Why do you think the agent continued his shtick without stopping? Well, my theory was that the agent wasn't seasoned enough to know when to stop. Sometimes the best advice you can give a new salesman is the power of shutting up. Ask a question, shut up and listen to the answer. Don't listen for an answer, listen to the answer. Well, anyways the agent tried writing down numbers and promising that the cash value of the life insurance policy would accumulate to a mere $5,000,000 in the span of 20 years' time...

What did I learn from this experience? Well, what did you learn? Take your time and don't be nervous. Why should you be nervous anyways? Let me give you a piece of advice that my second grade English teacher once gave me. Years ago, I was coerced to participate in a school play. To help me overcome my stage fright she said, "Mike don't be nervous. The audience only knows that you screwed up when you let them know you screwed up."

Presenting Too Many Offers

How many people want to walk onto a car lot and evaluate 100 different types' cars? Don't you have some idea of what you are looking for when you show up? When I sold my brokerage and starting shopping around for life insurance, it was an eye opening experience. Who is the expert? Most people need guidance and direction, don't steer but offer advice and a professional recommendation. Present the offer you feel is appropriate for the client and stay in your lane.

Not being prepared.

I once had a conversation with an agent friend of mine who was a day away from going on an advanced market case, bringing with him a point of sales consultant from the TPC. The need was for a buy/sell and other retirement products for a large business. I didn't realize that the agent was an expert for those products and was impressed that he got the appointment. When I asked he said, "I'm not an expert." To which I said, 'So what's your plan?" To which he replied, "I'm just going to read up about it the night before and kind of wing with having the consultant do most of the work..." To which, I said nothing and waited for the result. About a week later I followed up and the meeting did not go great. Preparation is half the battle with anything you do in life, people will expose you for what you truly are in this world. So, do your homework and prepare.

Throw the Kitchen Sink at em!

Don't throw the kitchen sink at your prospect! A client asks you for an opinion. What would you do if you were in my position? If it were me? I'd go with a permanent plan, because BLAH, BLAH AND BLAH. Look permanent insurance works in very selective situations with less price sensitive clients. Often we get eager when someone asks us for a recommendation to throw the entire kitchen sink. When a prospect would ask me something to that effect my answer was, 'I would go with a blended approach. I'd buy 30% permanent and 70% term insurance, where we can convert the term towards the end of the term into perm.' I take a very conservative approach to selling.

"A successful individual typically sets his next goal somewhat but not too much above his last achievement. In this way he steadily raises his level of aspiration." – Kurt Lewin

Chapter 12: Mindset of a Top Life Producer

What makes an MDRT level producer? What separates top life agents from the occasional term peddlers? The best life insurance producers will tell you that, 'Life insurance starts in the head then goes to the heart.' Life insurance sales is about finding and having a purpose. Uncovering beliefs and discovering what people care about the most. What are a person's priorities? Why should someone buy life insurance? From you?

Qualities of Top Producer

Habits

Habits can tell you a lot about a person. We all have habits, some good and some less desirable. The cool part about habits is that it involves a conscious choice to make a decision. What do you do when you wake up? How much time do you spend on social media per day? How often do you read about insurance per day?

Belief Systems

What do you believe insurance is for? I believe insurance is the greatest social good ever created and that we do make a real difference in our industry.

Activity

High performing life sales agents focus on activity driven life sales. If you sit around waiting for the phone to ring, you might have a lot of free time on your hands. The phone is powerful tool, pick it up and start using it.

Purpose

I'm convinced that there is not more powerful force for selling than having a compelling life story that drives your purpose. What drives you?

Own the concept, walks the walk

Do you actually believe what you sell to others? Do you own the concept? Are you providing advice that you would not or do not take? For me, my standard was always that I wanted to protect clients as well as I protected my grandmother.

Process

I'm a big fan of process oriented sales, this has not always been the case throughout my years of selling. A process makes selling incredibly easy, and it should be easy. Why not? What makes Mcdonald's so successful? Location? Food selection? It's a business that operates with such efficient systems that a 16 year old can manage a location.

Emotional about the concept and logical about the process.

Buying insurance should start with emotions and close on the process. The concept you sell should tethered to something important, what are you protecting? Why are you protecting it? Then focus on how we protect it.

Passion

Do you care? Do you care about what you do? If so, people will pick up on it. Talk about it and demonstrate it. I know passion and insurance sales do not often collide in the same sentences.

Goals

This isn't a motivation book. I'm not here to preach the gospel of work harder not smarter. This is a practical book for practical people and practical people need to set goals. Set yearly goals, set daily goals and track them.

Willpower

As a life agent you need to be willing to do what others will not be willing to do today, so you can have what others will not tomorrow. I'm a huge boxing fan and if you ever care to watch a great boxing bout, watch the Tyson Fury vs Deontay

Wilder heavyweight championship bout. Spoiler but fury gets knocked down, some people think knocked unconscious, and zombie-like wills himself back up off the canvas.

Having a Personal Story

My ex-business partner has one of the most powerful life insurance stories a person could have. Needless to say that it involves a tremendous amount of hardship placed upon a family member due to the bread winner not having life insurance.

"If you want truly to understand something, try to change it." – Kurt Lewin

Chapter 13: Thinking Outside the Box Techniques

Did you know that the odds of building a straight road through a rainforest is close to winning the lottery? Why do you think that might be? It's hard to get perspective on direction when in the forest, when we get lost in the woods. Once, I heard an interesting 'fact' that most people who get lost in the woods tend to die of shame, not the elements.

As salespeople we tend to be creative by nature, but we also tend to gravitate towards structure. Structure is great, don't get me wrong. But, too much structure can be a poison pill that destroys your personality. Think about your daily life, it's rife with structure. Is that bad? Not necessarily. Structure and repetitiveness is part of life, and it's the part of life that provides us with level of comfort.

How many times do you find yourself taking the exact same route home from work? Or, find yourself eating the same thing at the exact same restaurant? Have you ever found yourself watching television, and then the power goes out all of a sudden. To which, you keep watching a blank screen on your television. It happens. When trying to have that breakthrough moment for your practice, you will need to get out of your comfort zone. It's just like working out, you need to push yourself to grow.

Tips and Ideas

Here are some tips and ideas that I have used in the past to help think a bit outside of the box.

- Learn to have conversations without using placeholders such as, 'um'.
- Role play with other life agents.
- Secret Shop other life agents.
- Have conversations where you cannot say the word 'no'.
- Name recognition games
- Drive home from work and take an alternative route.
- Stand while you eat.
- Read a book every week.
- Read for 30 minutes per day.

I realize this chapter is rather lite, but what I want you to take away from this chapter is the fact that we fall into stable routines and for personal growth we need to mix things up once in a while.

"Experience alone does not create knowledge." –
Kurt Lewin

Chapter 14: Dealing with Stakeholders

Imagine if you would that you are forty-five minutes into what you thought was your greatest life insurance presentation and all of a sudden the prospect interrupts you by asking, "I should really run this by my accountant first." How do you overcome objections from key stakeholders? What's your strategy? Aside from family these are your three largest obstacles for permanent insurance. Or I like to call them the Triple A's:

- Accountants
- Attorneys
- Advisors

So, how do we handle the Triple A's? As life agents these stakeholders for the most part have been primed to think a certain way about life insurance. What do I mean? Let's break them down.

Accountants

Accountants are not all the same. That being said, generally speaking accountants are all about what? The numbers. The numbers show that term insurance over a client's general life span is about 10X less expensive. This is a somewhat true statement. Why? Because, ultimately for a term insurance program to work over the long term, what does that require? It requires the insured to be insurable. It requires the insured to remain in consistent good health until age 70! It requires no accidents, no mishaps and no surprises in the life of the insured from age 20 to age 70!

Attorneys

Lawyers are typically very strong advocates for insurance. Why? Because, they have to be three dimensional thinkers and very open minded. Don't overlook attorneys as referral partners.

Advisors

Advisors have counter agendas to insurance. The goal of an advisor is to maximize wealth. How does the advisor get paid? By commission or by a percentage fee per year. The more the advisor grows the asset pool, the more the advisor gets paid. This is why, predominately advisors spout, "Buy Term and Invest the difference." After watching one of my favorite financial advisor crush an old married couple on their whole life purchase decision, I thought to really start writing about how financial advisors are just plain wrong. Why are they wrong? In the case of the 80 year old married couple, whole life was the correct choice. Why? Well Mike, if the couple invested the difference then they would have had a lot more built up than the insurance policy. There are three faulty assumptions advisors make with that statement.

1. The insured no longer qualified for term insurance due to age and health, so the term would have been un-used and wasted money.
2. No one ever invests the difference, although we all say we would.
3. The couple could have lost all of that 'difference' in a stock market crash.

Look, aside from those 3 key faulty assumptions. The insurance policy is probably earning around 3 or 4% and you can take a loan against it tax free. So, we should invest and risk all the difference knowing for a few percentage points? Let's be honest when some financial advisors say that insurance agents have no business helping make investment decisions, they might not be completely wrong. Have you ever heard, "Insurance and investments should remain different things, insurance is insurance and investments are investments."

The Triple A Workaround

Well Mike, how do I get around the Triple A? Honestly, there is no way to get around them. You need to work with them and get them on the side of the client. Your recommendation just like their recommendation should hold equal weight, but it won't in the eyes of the client. Don't avoid hard conversations, embrace them. All three of the triple A's know their domain, but how well do they understand your domain? Probably, not much more than the typical person you speak with. What if you could make it a collaborative experience and not a combative experience? Wouldn't that be something? Bring them to the table. For instance, "Before we start Jim, are you the person who normally makes this decision? What I mean is do you consult with anyone else?"

"Twenty years from now you will be more disappointed by the things that you didn't do than by the ones you did do."-Mark Twain

Chapter 15: Conclusion

Why did you read this book? What made you pick it up? Why did you become an insurance agent? As you pursue your insurance career, remember to be resolute in your commitment to keeping your commitments. The fact that you took the time to read this book tells me something about the kind of person you aspire to be. Why did you pick up insurance sales? What was the reason? To what end? What is your goal? What is your compelling vision of the future? Selling life insurance is a rather simple process, but where most of us run into trouble is in the marketing and prospecting arena.

A lot of this information might have seemed a bit preachy, because it was meant to be. I know what you're saying, "Come on Mike, would you really say that to a client?" The answer is resoundingly yes, but it depends on the client and on the rapport. Each situation is different and requires the finesse of the broker to make a judgment call. Not all clients will have the tolerance to have a DIMES conversation or want to disclose information to a life agent. Some clients want a quick quote and nothing more. It's important to understand and assess the specific needs and wants of each client on an individual basis.

Every sales book is going to be a little

different, my style in particular involves putting a lot back on the client and having a thoughtful conversation about needs. A lot of sales trainers will tell you that the excitement is in the negotiating and closing. For me, having that thoughtful conversation and preventing objections is the juice. Take what you can from this book that you find useful and discard the rest. Sherlock Holmes once compared the memory to an attic and eventually that attic gets full of stuff, so some things must get removed to accommodate new ideas. As far as phrasing, re-phrase the questions to suit your needs or take pieces of them that you find useful.

Index of Questions

Transition

- By the way who do you have your life insurance with?
- Who's your life insurance with? (Is that important to you?)
- Would it surprise you to know that about 50% of my clients end up paying nothing out of pocket for their long term care insurance?
  - o Using a simple strategy.
- Could your spouse pay off your home if you were to pass away? (That way you don't have to give it back to the bank or move.)
- God forbid if something were to happen to you how much would your family need each year to maintain the same standard of living and how much would you need to give them a higher standard of living. How olds your youngest and set up your income replacement for 20 years.
- Now that we have insured your assets, let's talk about what is truly important, what's protecting your loved ones from financial ruin?

Have you ever thought about mortgage protection insurance?

- Have you ever thought about life insurance?
- If I could better protect your family would you consider buying better life insurance?
- How much life insurance coverage do you have to protect your family?
- Did you know our company offers an auto discount if you also have life insurance? (With the company)
- Prospect, when was the last time you got your blood tested or had a check-up? (Never used myself but heard it works from a successful broker, target is 50 YO men)
- I noticed you don't have life insurance with us who's it with?
- Have you met with our agency's life insurance specialist?
- Have you taken advantage of you free life insurance reviews?

Business Owner

- What type of succession plan do you have in place?

○ What can you tell me about it?

- Who are your key employees? The kind that are irreplaceable?
- What kind of plan do you have in place to protect your business in case something should happen to them?

General Asset Annuity Opportunity Probing

- Do you have any other assets that act as life insurance?
- Do you have any assets that you would want to pass along?
- What do you have that acts like life insurance? What I mean is, what do you currently have that if god forbid you were to pass away, would pass on to your loved ones?

Wants Assessment – Price Sensitivity

- Ideally, what would you like your plan to look like?
- Have you ever thought about paying in full for your insurance?

Urgency Seed Planting Question

- If something were to happen to you today, walking out of this office. What would it take to pay off the remainder of your mortgage, roughly speaking?

Death Benefit currently Too low

- How did you come up with that amount of insurance?
- How did you come up with this plan? (Poke a hole in the plan, attack the plan not the price to compete against the current agent, credibility beats price)

Value Question

- How often do you meet with your current agent/broker to make sure your protection meets your current needs? (Use this to dilute their current agents value and assess needs or wants)

DIMES Question

- Do you own this home? (This is a Kurt way of asking, so be careful. I never like to assume) – Close Ended

- Can your spouse pay off the house if you pass away? (That way you don't have to give the house back to the bank or move.)
- What kind of assists are we looking to protect? – Open Ended
- If something were to happen to you how much would it take today to pay off the mortgage?
- Do you want your kids to attend Harvard or Yale? Stole this from Shawshank Redemption.
- If something were to happen to you who would pay off your student loans?
- If something were to happen to you today, walking out of this office. What would it take to pay off the remainder of your mortgage, roughly speaking?
- What do you think it costs to attend college these days? If you were to guess?
  o What about when Billy turns 18 in 2035?
- Do you have other assets that you are going to pass along?

Other Insurance Questions

- Do you have any insurance at work?
- How long have you had it for?

- What can you tell me about it?

Micro Close

- Is that something you want coverage/protection for?

Group Life / Company Policy Rebuttal Questions

- That's great! When did you get that policy? (Work policy)
- That's great! When did you get that policy?"
- "That's great! Why don't we set some time aside this week to review it?"

No time Rebuttal Question

- *John, if we could put together a great policy/package to protect your family, would you give us 15-20 minutes?*

Needs Assessment Probing

- Did you know how much insurance you needed? Or were you looking for some guidance?
- Did you have an idea of how much insurance you wanted? Or would you like some guidance?

- Do you have any other assets that act like life insurance? (That pass along to loved ones)
- Have you ever considered paying for your insurance in full?
- Would you consider paying in full if you could get a significant discount?
- How would you like to pay?

22423005R00063

Made in the USA
San Bernardino, CA
12 January 2019